SOAR
WITH THE
EAGLES

Principles, Practices, and
Insightful Stories to Help You
Achieve Your Hopes and Dreams

Walter D. Smith

Management Strategies, Inc.

ACKNOWLEDGMENTS

I am eternally grateful for the blessing of my wonderful wife Yvonne and our six children: Michele, Michael, Kevin, Bryan, Denise, and Derek.

I cherish their love and affection more than words can say. Each of them has inspired me in countless ways by their individual achievements, strong sense of personal responsibility, and devotion to God, family, friends, and country.

Thanks are in order for Jim Rohn, America's foremost business philosopher, and Mark Victor Hansen, co-author of the "Chicken Soup" books, for inspiring me to write this book. For their encouragement and help, I thank Jack Pachuta, speaker, author, and consultant and Ron Gabrielsen (The Cold Call Man), speaker, trainer, author, and consultant. For their help in drafting and editing the stories herein, my thanks go to Derek Smith and Marnie Krainik.

I also thank all the great people, known and unknown, who are mentioned in this book. I hope the observations and experiences shared herein positively influence your life as much as they have influenced mine.

CONTENTS

INTRODUCTION

Throughout life, each of us is presented with a variety of challenges, seen by some people as problems. In this book, challenges are correctly described as opportunities.

Whether ultimately harmful or helpful, the impact of challenges is determined by how you deal with them. If you view them as problems, chances are the final results will be less than satisfactory.

This book examines a number of challenges you may very well face in your own personal or business life. Others have successfully dealt with these challenges, and their solutions are shared with you. By referencing and adopting their techniques, you won't spend the time and incur the cost of reinventing the total solution. Instead, you will have a head start and will address your challenges and pursue your *hopes and dreams* with greater confidence.

Hopes and Dreams - Those positive, powerful forces that help us look to the future with full faith and confidence that tomorrow will be better than today.

--Walter D. Smith

FOREWORD

The concept of "Hopes and Dreams" is not new. In the Bible, Isaiah 40:31, it says: "But those who wait on the Lord shall renew their strength, they shall mount up with wings like eagles, they shall run and not be weary, and they shall walk and not faint."

Throughout the centuries, *hopes and dreams* have inspired and motivated people to stay the course during periods of darkness, depression, and near despair. Individuals with a positive sense of direction have always been encouraged by their *hopes and dreams.*

Hope - a feeling that what is wanted will happen; it is desire accompanied by expectation.

Dream - a fond hope or aspiration which is thought of as being desirable and possible.

Together, *hopes and dreams* are feelings that what you want is desirable and possible and that it will happen. Your *hopes and dreams* can become reality!

Some people in life become victims. Others become victors. In most of life's challenges you influence the final outcome by choices you make and actions you take. In this book, you'll read about people believing in their *hopes and dreams* and taking the positive steps that made them victors.

No one in recent times better articulated, nor better demonstrated, the power of *hopes and dreams* than the late Dr. Martin Luther King.

In his powerful "I Have a Dream" speech, Dr. King said, "I have a dream . . .,""This is our hope . . ." and he went on to talk about freedom and his *hopes and dreams*, concluding with, "For when we let freedom ring, we will speed up that day when all of God's children, black men and white men, Jews and Gentiles, Protestants and Catholics will be able to join hands and sing in the words of that old Negro spiritual, 'Free at last, free at last, thank God almighty, we are free at last.'"

Dr. King changed the course of history by releasing and activating *hopes and dreams* that had long been imprisoned in the hearts, souls, and minds of many men, women, and children - of all races, colors, and creeds.

Although Dr. King's *hopes and dreams* have not become a total reality, much progress has been made. It is important to recognize and understand the enduring, positive, powerful force of Dr. King's *hopes and dreams*. Is there something in your life you want to improve - your personal relationships with spouse, significant others, family, or friends, your job, your health, your finances, your lifestyle, or other troubling situation?

An attitude and commitment like Dr. King's and the

application of the principles and techniques described and illustrated in the following chapters can make your *hopes and dreams* come true.

CONFIDENCE

Confidence comes not from always being right but from not fearing to be wrong.

-- Peter T. McIntyre

THE PROCESS
OF CHANGE

Whether managing a business or our lives, certain, basic principles and behavior patterns contribute to success. For starters, you must ask yourself a series of questions - an inquiry process to form a framework for action.

(a) What is the current status of the object of your inquiry? That is, company sales, company profits, your weight, your salary, your hopes, or your dreams?

(b) What do you want the status to be?

(c) What will you do to affect the changes to get from where you are to where you want to be?

(d) How will you make those changes?

(e) Who can help you make the changes?

(f) When will you implement the actions to make the changes?

(g) What is your timetable?

After you perform that analysis and create your *plan*, you must then constantly monitor where you are relative to where you should be according to your timetable.

Each of us could prepare an extensive list of individuals who have successfully applied these principles. To illustrate the process, the success of one individual quickly comes to mind. His story is shared with you in the next chapter.

FOCUS

Establish your goals and concentrate your energy and talent totally to accomplishing them. That is how to achieve success. Focus is essential.

A Chinese Proverb says, "A man who chases two rabbits catches neither."

PLANNING, PRACTICE, PATIENCE, PERSISTENCE

Charles "Chick" Linster

To achieve his *hopes and dreams,* Chick followed the classic format for success. His story illustrates the processes of *planning, practice, patience,* and *persistence.*

Chick's ultimate dream was an extension of the success he achieved in physical fitness when he was only 13 years old and answered the challenge of President John F. Kennedy's Council on Physical Fitness.

As part of Chick's plan, he established a daily regimen of exercises which included a targeted number of pushups, situps, chinups, and jumping jacks. He set a specified number of repetitions for each exercise - the process of quantification. Establishing a number, he was able to measure and monitor his progress.

As a high school freshman, Chick participated in the physical education test that included proficiency in pushups, pullups, the standing long jump, a half-mile run, and the stride-straddle hop, an agility test. His 123 pushups and total score of 657 points approached the school records of 126 pushups and 667 total points.

Chick posted the highest scores in the high school for that year. His competitors were other freshmen plus sophomores, juniors, and seniors. Chick outperformed them all.

But, he didn't say, "Now I have proven myself, I quit." Instead, he was disappointed. He had established himself as the best for that year but fell short of the school records.

Chick was *persistent* in the pursuit of his *hopes and dreams*. He worked out daily and increased his repetitions in each exercise, while establishing a rigorous *practice* schedule.

Remember, Chick's experience illustrates the use and benefits of *planning, practice, patience*, and *persistence*. Chick knew he could not go from one pushup to thousands overnight. He was *patient* and created a master *plan* with a *practice* schedule that quantified his goal and established a timetable for his *practice* sessions. He then had to hang in there - to *persist* in carrying out his *plan* no matter what obstacles intervened. He overcame the obstacles and moved forward to realize his *hopes and dreams*.

Maybe I'm jumping the gun, but you've got to know what happened. As a freshman, you'll recall Chick barely fell short of the school records of 126 pushups and 667 total points. The next year, he shattered them by completing 1,000 pushups and accumulating 4,100 total points!

He *planned, practiced,* was *patient,* and *persistent.* As a result, he improved significantly with respective increases of 713% and 524%.

How much closer would you be to your *hopes and dreams* (goals) if you improved your current performance by 713% or even 524%? And, if you could do it in only one year, wouldn't that be marvelous? Depending on the magnitude of your goals, with diligent creation of your *plan* and disciplined *practice, patience, and persistence,* many of them could probably be realized in less than a year.

Here is more about Chick's successful application of *planning, practice, patience,* and *persistence.* Let's examine how he achieved worldwide recognition by making another dream come true.

During his preparation for the physical fitness test, Chick discovered he was good at doing pushups. However, the difference between his best and worst efforts was significant. To correct that, he intensified his daily workouts, steadily increasing his personal best for consecutive pushups from the 123 performed in the freshman competition to 222, 333, and 444 as he continued to adjust his plan and raise his goal. To continue to improve, or to maximize your potential at anything, you must, like Chick, raise your standards once you have achieved a goal.

At age 14, Chick defined one of his biggest dreams - to set the world pushup record and have it recognized and published in The Guinness Book of World Records. He did not know the consecutive pushup record. However, he had heard someone on a TV show claim a total of 3,000 pushups. With that number as a guideline, he quantified his goal and pursued his dream.

Chick kept reaching and raising his goal for consecutive pushups. Finally, he did 3,003 pushups exceeding what he thought was the record. Only then did he hear that a Marine had done 5,000 consecutive pushups. That news could have dashed the dream of a less-driven and ambitious person.

Chick again took measure of where he was, where he had to go, what he had to do to get there, and what was a reasonable schedule.

Chick then revised his *practice* schedule. He continually increased his number of repetitions until he had established a two-tier schedule. On school days when he needed to reserve time for studying, he did 1,750 consecutive pushups. On weekends when he had more time, he did 3,000 consecutive pushups each day.

Chick's dad, Richard, told me that where Chick practiced his pushups in front of the TV, Chick's perspiration had created an outline of his body on the carpet. Richard said that he eventually removed the carpeting and put down tile. I don't know whether or not Richard was serious, but putting down tile seemed like a pretty good idea to me.

Finally, in the fall of his junior year in high school, Chick decided to try for the world pushup record. To validate it as an official record, it was necessary for him to have witnesses to verify the count and to certify that the pushups were done correctly and consecutively - nonstop!

At 3:08 p.m. with witnesses in place, Chick began his first pushup. At about 4,000 pushups, a scab on Chick's elbow broke loose causing blood to trickle down his arm and pool by his wrist, but Chick pressed on. *Persistence*!!!

At 7:02 p.m., three hours and 54 minutes after he began, Chick's coach forced him to stop. He did 6,006 consecutive, perfectly executed pushups, achieving his dream and establishing a world record that was preserved for history in <u>The Guinness Book of World Records</u>.

When Chick told me about his record-setting performance, he said that he was confident he could have done 7,000 and wanted to keep going. But, Chick's sides were getting raw from being brushed by his arms as he went up and down, and the coach said he stopped the effort because of his concern for Chick's physical condition. Chick jokingly said, "I think he stopped me because he was hungry. After all, it was after 7:00 p.m."

Chick set the world record two and a half years after he defined his dream and began his preparation. That speaks volumes for the power of a well-conceived *plan* accompanied by *practice, patience* and *persistence.*

Preparing for his world record-setting performance, Chick performed over 1,100,000 pushups. His world renowned accomplishment speaks well of the benefit of *practice.* Among his benefits were physical stamina, endurance, and confidence.

I could write a book about Charles "Chick" Linster. It is my intent to share just enough to help you gain some guidance and inspiration to help you in the pursuit of your *hopes and dream.*

Someday, Chick may decide to write his own book. He is the man, and it is his story.

After a telephone call, Chick sent me a wealth of information about his dream and how it came true. As part of the memo sent with his notes, he wrote, "Dear Walt: I have attached a copy of my account on how I set the world pushup record and what it meant to me. Please use it as you see fit."

It is appropriate that, here and now, I express my gratitude to Chick for the encouragement and inspiration for me and the thousands of people to whom I have told his story. I am greatly indebted to him for allowing me to share it with you.

"... 6,004, 6,005, 6,006."

Postscript

I must share with you a couple more insights about Chick and the kind of person he is. The next section about "attitude" could very well include his story of positive *attitude*. However, this entire opening section is dedicated to Chick, so his *attitude* is shared with you now.

A little more than two months after establishing the world pushup record, Chick broke his neck during gymnastics practice and was permanently paralyzed. In speaking of the accident he says, "Then disaster struck. In the twinkling of an eye, my body and world were shattered. However, since I had trained, worked, and sacrificed for a seemingly purposeless exploit, I was able to redirect this effort toward my rehabilitation. I salvaged as much of my body as possible and rebuilt my world. I found a practical application for the Ulysses factor." The Ulysses factor is a theory that there is some factor in man, some form of special adaptation, that prompts a few individuals to exploits that may seem purposeless but are ultimately a value to the race.

Since his accident, Chick's indomitable will and spirit have enabled him to overcome more adversity, successfully rise to significant challenges, and realize more dreams. We will reserve those stories for him to tell in his book.

Chick's Positive Attitude

A few years ago, Chick and I were together at a wedding reception. Sitting across the table from me in his wheelchair, he told me about how lucky he was. I asked why he would say that. He said, "You know Walt, before my accident, it was my plan to enlist in the Marines when I graduated from high school. It was my goal to be the best Marine in the entire Marine Corps.

Since my injury, I have had lots of time to think. I have determined that had I not been injured and joined the Marines as planned, I would have been in Vietnam about the time of the Tet Offensive. As you know, that was not a good battle for our troops. I could have come home in worse shape than I am in - or maybe even in a pine box. Yes, I am very lucky."

Thanks Again, Chick

PRACTICE - PRACTICE - PRACTICE

It is said that practice makes perfect. However, unless we constantly fine-tune and improve our techniques and skills, we merely become perfect (perhaps just very good) at our present level of performance.

Yes, it is possible to improve our ability to do something poorly. Unfortunately, continued practice at a substandard level eventually becomes an ingrained acceptance, and we are reluctant to change. So, when we accept the suggestion to practice, practice, practice, let us make sure our practice is accompanied by improvement.

ATTITUDE

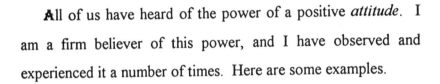

All of us have heard of the power of a positive *attitude*. I am a firm believer of this power, and I have observed and experienced it a number of times. Here are some examples.

Mamie Dawkins

Although I have never met her, Mamie is one of my heroines. Mamie embodies the best of what makes a dedicated, dependable, loyal employee and co-worker, but most important, an admirable human being.

Mamie is a lady who lived on the far south side of Chicago. She arose every morning at 3 a.m. and boarded a bus at 4 a.m. to arrive at her job at a downtown Chicago hotel by 6 a.m. Mamie was not late and did not call in sick in over 39 years of employment.

Near the end of her working career, Mamie was assigned to a new position. She transferred to the hotel laundry.

In response to an inquiry as to how she liked her new job, Mamie said she liked it very well - much better than her old job of making beds and cleaning rooms all day.

What an *attitude*! Do you think her positive outlook on life and its challenges strengthened Mamie as she boarded that bus at 4 a.m. every morning? I believe it did. When I am tempted to think I have it tough, thoughts of Mamie's positive *attitude* and its application strengthen me.

Boarded Bus at 4 a.m.

Denise

Denise is a young lady who had a traumatic experience at age 16. She had a brain hemorrhage! At the time, she was a member of the varsity football cheerleading squad, an all-around (4 event) gymnast, and at the top of her class academically.

She lapsed into a coma and surgery was delayed for several days because of swelling in her brain. Despite the delay, doctors predicted that within hours after surgery she would be walking, talking, and performing rather normally.

It didn't happen that way. She remained in a comatose state for weeks and, subsequently, underwent extensive rehabilitation to restore some basic life skills such as feeding herself. But, she didn't give up. She did what she had to do.

A good portion of her junior year of high school was spent in recovery and rehabilitation. With help from her guidance counselor, special tutors, and many other people, she completed her junior year just days before the beginning of her senior year in high school. She did graduate with her class. Her grade point average was only three-tenths of a point behind the class valedictorian. She ranked third in her class but said that was okay, because she didn't want to make a speech anyway.

As it was, Denise received a standing ovation from her classmates when she accepted her diploma. Her fellow students knew she had successfully fought a tough battle and won.

What does all of this have to do with *attitude*? Well, there's a lot more to this story including a second brain surgery that had not been anticipated. Before she left home for the second surgery, Denise cut a small heart out of red construction paper. On the heart she wrote, "Dear Mom and Dad, please don't worry about me. I know I have your full love and support. And besides, when the going gets tough, I don't quit!" She left the note on her parents' nightstand. It was discovered after she had gone to the hospital. How's that for *attitude*?

At the hospital, the parents of another young patient asked Denise, "Don't you ever get angry with God and ask why he struck you down during your prime when you were a football cheerleader, an all-around gymnast, and an academic leader of your class?'"

Denise replied, "No, I don't think that way. I know things like this happen to people in life. It may as well happen to me as to someone who can't handle it." Do you think her positive *attitude* and faith helped Denise with her recovery?

At the hospital, many people referred to her as "the Miracle Girl." In its annual Christmas card, the hospital profiled Denise. The column was headed "From St. Mary's to Prom Queen . . . ."

Denise's story was published in <u>Possibilities</u> (The Magazine of Hope) under the title of "From Coma to Overcomer: I never thought to ask, `Why me, God?'"

By now, you have probably concluded much more could be written about Denise. You are absolutely correct. I state that with a reasonable amount of certainty, because Denise's last name is Smith. She is my youngest daughter. Someday, I hope to meet you, and I will tell you all you want to know.

Displaying her positive *attitude* and making the best of a painful, life-changing experience, Denise said, "Looking back, I think this whole experience has made me a better person, a more compassionate person. I can empathize and talk with people who are fighting similar battles."

How about you? Will you help someone who is fighting a battle? Your kindness will be appreciated and returned many times over.

"I Never Thought to Ask, 'Why Me, God?'"

Jeremiah A. Denton, Jr.

Commander Denton was a Navy pilot flying a mission over Vietnam when his plane was shot down. He was captured and subsequently spent seven and a half years as a prisoner in various camps including the infamous Hanoi Hilton.

From what I have heard and read of the prison camps, I am sure Commander Denton endured much physical and emotional pain and suffering. Despite his own discomfort, he never shunned his duty to his country or his leadership responsibilities to his countrymen who were imprisoned with him.

At a televised Vietnamese propaganda event, Commander Denton and several other prisoners were prominently displayed before the television cameras. The enemy's objective was to show the world how well the American prisoners were being treated and how healthy and well-cared-for they looked.

That portrayal was not accurate. Commander Denton wanted the world to know the truth. Using his eyes and Morse code, he blinked out the message that the prisoners were being tortured. That's a bit of insight to the man. How about his *attitude*?

While imprisoned, Commander Denton was promoted to Captain. Captain Denton was with the first plane load of prisoners flown out of Vietnam after their release. Upon deplaning at Clark Field in the Philippines, Captain Denton spotted an American flag. He came to attention, saluted the flag, and said, "God Bless America." Later, he made the observation that he and the men returning with him were honored to have had the opportunity to serve their country during a time of great difficulty.

Captain Denton's patriotism and desire to serve his country were not diminished by his Vietnam experience. After his retirement from the Navy, he served as a United States Senator from the State of Alabama. He also founded and worked tirelessly for United Families of America.

I met (then) Senator Denton a few years ago in Washington, D.C. Our visit was very brief - less than five minutes. However, I was compelled to thank him. I expressed my gratitude to him and his family for the pain, suffering, and loneliness they endured in their service to our country.

Again, revealing a great *attitude*, and modesty, he told me he was only doing his duty. And, speaking of his imprisonment, he said that he wasn't the only one there, conveying, but not saying, that many American service men endured the same experience, and he didn't consider himself special.

Do you think a strong faith and positive *attitude* helped keep Senator Denton going during the tough times of his life?

How could a brighter, more positive outlook improve your life today? Brighten your outlook and polish it regularly. You will be amazed at the results.

"I Wasn't the Only One There."

BE BRAVE

A coward dies a thousand deaths a brave man dies but one.

The Cat

Lessons on attitude and behavior are all around us. Even a cat reaffirmed some of my beliefs about strength of character and courage. To fully appreciate the significance of my learning from a cat, there are some things you should know.

I am not a fancier of cats. With one short-term exception, we never had cats as pets in my parents' home. In fact, we children were always warned to keep babies away from cats, and vice versa, because cats "suck the breath" out of babies and suffocate them.

Also, it was always a dog, not a cat, that was man's best friend. This seemed to be true because we often saw owners walking with their dogs or driving around with the dog sitting on the seat as if it owned the vehicle. You just don't see chummy relationships like that with cats.

About thirteen years ago, one of our children received a cat as a gift from a friend. The child is grown and long gone from the house, but the cat remains. This cat is named Tatum. Like most cats, Tatum is very independent. She sleeps a lot and pretty much does what she wants to do, how she wants to do it, and when she wants to do it.

When she was younger, Tatum added to my learned dislike of cats by scratching my children whom I regarded more highly than any cat. She also sharpened her claws on the furniture. I wasn't too happy having a cat wreck furniture I had worked hard to purchase. Needless to say, her independent attitude and destructive actions did nothing to change my feelings toward cats.

However, that did not keep me from learning a thing or two by watching her. A couple of years ago, she had a kidney removed. A few months after that, she climbed under the hood of my wife's van. When my son left the house and started the van, there was a thumping and banging under the hood.

Tatum was slammed to the concrete driveway under the car. She was stripped of some fur, and she had several ugly gashes on her body. A fair number of stitches was required to sew her up.

HERE COMES THE LESSON as I saw it. Her life was endangered in both the kidney illness and the accident. Yet, she persevered and survived them both. During the recovery processes, she dragged herself around as best she could and continued to practice her independent nature. Impressive to me was that, contrary to what is sometimes individual human nature, she *didn't whine and whimper* about her pain and misfortune. She took matters into her own paws and did things her way. I admired "her way."

Tatum is a bit older and mellower now. Although we still have some differences of opinion about how she does some things, it is safe to say that we have become chums. She's probably the only cat with whom I'll ever have a warm relationship. After all, there most likely will never be another cat that will take thirteen years to train me.

"I'll Do It My Way."

MOVE ON

Even during good times, you will experience painful challenges. Do the best you can and move on with your life.

--Walter D. Smith

IMPRESSIONS

A well-known and often repeated phrase is that you only have one chance to make a good first *impression*. There's no question that the *impressions* you make will greatly influence your life. The *impressions* may be negative or positive. Since this book is intended to provide positive thoughts and suggestions for your consideration, I will share with you just a few powerful, positive first *impressions*.

General George S. Patton

My knowledge of General Patton is limited to what I have read, war movies, news reports I saw during World War II, and a statement by General Patton I read while visiting a military museum at Fort Benning, Georgia.

It occurred to me that our first *impressions* take many forms - physical, verbal, and written. General Patton said, "I am a soldier. I fight where I am told. I win where I fight." Fifteen small words with a total of only 44 letters, but they speak volumes about the man - General Patton.

Here is my analysis of that statement and the *impressions* made on me.

"I am a soldier." - General Patton was proud of what he was, a soldier, and the manner in which he chose to serve his country.

"I fight where I am told." - The General respected authority. He obeyed orders and did what he had to do wherever he had to do it.

"I win where I fight." - General Patton had confidence in himself, his superiors, his peers, and his subordinates.

Although the General was prepared to surrender his life in combat, he didn't expect that to happen, and if it did - his troops would do whatever was necessary to win the day. He would win - dead or alive.

Had I met him in person, I am sure General Patton would have made a strong, favorable first *impression* no matter what form it took.

"I am a Soldier."

BE PREPARED

I have studied the enemy all of my life. I know exactly how he will react under any given set of circumstances. And he hasn't the slightest idea what I'm going to do.

So when the time comes, I'm going to whip the hell out of him.

--General George S. Patton

An Athlete

A few years ago, I attended a meeting of business managers in Waterloo, Iowa. A prominent athlete was the keynote speaker for the evening.

After the thought-provoking, informative presentation, the crowd of 300 managers descended on the speaker to meet him and get his autograph. I am not keen on standing in line or being stepped on, pushed around, or shoved. So, I wasn't part of the crowd that stampeded the speaker.

However, I too wanted to meet him and obtain his autograph. So, I just wandered around the meeting facility socializing for about an hour and a half. By then, it was after 10 p.m.

At the time, my wife and I had five children and my brother-in-law (a track coach and former track star) and sister-in-law had four children. I approached the speaker with ten small slips of paper.

By now, the speaker was alone, except for me, and probably eager to head for home. I said to him, "Sir, I know you have had a long day, it is after 10 p.m., and you have a long drive back to Chicago. However, I have a small favor to ask of you. Will you just autograph these 10 slips of paper as fast as you can?" Graciously, making a good third or forth *impression*, he said, "No, no, no - we'll not do it that way. Let's do it right. Who will be receiving these autographs?"

I provided him the names. He then took ten larger slips of paper and personalized each autograph as follows:

> To Michele - Most Sincerely
>
> To Mike - Best of Luck
>
> To Kevin - Good Luck
>
> To Bryan - My Kindest Regards
>
> To Denise - My Sincere Greetings

plus what he wrote to DuWayne, Debbie, Kim, Peggy, and Greg.

By the way, he signed his name - JESSE OWENS.

Mr. Owens did pretty well for a fellow from Alabama who at age seven was picking cotton and working to meet a quota of 100 pounds a day. Many *hopes and dreams* must have been fulfilled as he worked his way from the cotton fields to four Olympic gold medals and then to national public relations counselor for six firms.

Jesse Owens left his indelible *impression* on millions of

people and scores of record books.

"Let's do it Right."

A Little Boy

Our discussion of first *impressions* would be woefully incomplete if I failed to note that actions, words, and deeds can create a first *impression* that doesn't properly reflect the spirit, heart, and soul of the individual. The moral of that observation - don't rush to judgment. If the situation permits, take a little time and form your first *impression* slowly. That lesson was reaffirmed for me a few months ago by an eleven-year-old fifth grader.

I was invited to participate in National Reading Month by reading to a class of students. I have assisted with this project for a number of years, and I have had many great experiences. An example is hugs from little first graders who, I am told, don't get many hugs at home. That gives me a warm, fuzzy feeling and a real sense of doing something worthwhile. Maybe not really big and significant, but definitely worthwhile. However, in the lives of those little children, maybe the experience is big and significant. If so, I am pleased to have been a part of it.

Whoops, back to this year and the fifth graders. The focus of my reading is eagles. We read and talk of the characteristics of eagles - their speed, eyesight, hunting skills, beauty, independence, and other skills, and how we can learn from eagles. We discuss how each of us can develop our minds and bodies so that we can do whatever we want to do and be whatever we want to be.

Believe me, it is an exciting, stirring, high energy session. That being the case, I always anticipate rapt attention and eager involvement by the students. They don't disappoint me.

This day with the fifth graders was going well except for the first *impression* I was forming of one eleven-year-old boy. As I conducted my interesting, provocative, and inspiring (take my word for it, please) session, this little fellow seemed preoccupied with something on his desk.

I knew it wasn't me, so I began to wonder - what's wrong with him? How can I get to him? What story should I tell next? What questions should I ask him? What changes should I make in my gestures, my vocal variety? What else could I do?

At the end of the one-hour class, rumpled, exhausted, and worn out, I still had not captured this boy's undivided attention. By then, self doubt had started to creep in, and I was wondering whether this boy would ever amount to anything in life.

Then, my nemesis for the day, little Ben Kieffer, stepped forward and burned into my consciousness the wisdom of not being too quick to form first *impressions.*

Ben stepped forward and handed me a sheet of paper. He said, "Here, Mr. Smith, I drew a picture of an eagle for you."

"I Drew a Picture of an Eagle for You."

For your personal success and happiness, work to make every *impression* a good *impression*. When I visit with young people, I give them this plastic chip to aid them with their positive reinforcement.

BE
KEEN OF VISION
SHARP OF MIND
SWIFT TO ACT

WALT SMITH
PROFESSIONAL SPEAKER
608-356-7733
® 1990

INTEGRITY

The Used Car Salesman

When professionals in my field are hired, the client frequently is in financial trouble. This particular engagement was no exception.

The client had been a very successful auto dealer. He owned the largest and most profitable dealership in his region of the USA. His success allowed him to be very charitable with his time and money.

When astronauts returned from space, this fellow provided convertibles for use in the huge parades organized to welcome them home. As I remember, he had several children, yet he made room for the homeless.

At the time, many Vietnamese families were fleeing to the United States. This car dealer made available one of his homes for the immigrants. By any measure, this man was an outstanding human being.

When I came aboard as a consultant, his business was

in serious trouble. Auto sales had declined significantly and the dealership had been forced to relocate to a smaller facility in a less desirable location.

The financial institutions were constantly badgering the owner. When a vehicle was sold, he couldn't close the deal until he obtained a release from the bank. This sometimes became very awkward and embarrassing.

I was impressed by this man's faith. He went to church every day. On the wall across from his desk hung a plaque bearing this message: "If a man believes in himself and his God, he will never be permanently defeated."

This man was admirable because of his character and *integrity*. He chose to solve his problems with hard, honest work.

During the engagement, I learned that his father-in-law was a ranking member of the Mafia. I had assisted federal courts and the Treasury Department in audits of Mafia scams, and was familiar with mysterious fires and intimidation tactics that were often used to solve problems like my client's.

Yes, he had great integrity. When I moved away to join a large company, this client was still fighting his way back to financial stability -- one automobile at a time!

One Automobile at a Time

DON'T PITY YOU

When the going is rough and life seems unfair, do not throw a pity party for yourself; the benefits to you are minimal, and your family, friends, and neighbors can do without adding your burdens to theirs.

--Walter D. Smith

GRACE and STRENGTH

The eagle soars

the eagle glides;

It does not run

it does not hide.

The eagle flies high

for all to see;

A symbol of strength

for you and me.

NICE

I have discovered that an otherwise rough day can be improved by *nice* people. By *nice*, I mean pleasant, kind, considerate. A fellow named Thompson said, "Be kind to everyone you meet for everyone is fighting a battle." As I experience more of life's challenges and observe the burdens borne by some people, I am increasingly convinced of the truth in Thompson's statement.

Volumes could be written about individuals who have performed major and minor *nice* deeds that have made a difference in my life. I will spare you the volumes and share only a few.

Lady at the Train Station

The impact of this event was obviously very great as it occurred over 30 years ago. In my warm memory of the *nice* lady, it seems like only yesterday.

At the time, I was an officer of a worldwide company that

was headquartered in downtown Chicago, Illinois. I commuted by train between Chicago and my home which was about 40 miles west.

The train trip home began at Union Station, where I arrived late one evening after the large crowds were gone. I then discovered I had misplaced my wallet and had no money for the fare.

Being resourceful, I wasn't too concerned. Although I was reluctant to do so, I felt, if worse came to worse, I could call home (reversing the charges) and ask my wife to come for me. With six children under age nine, that was not an attractive alternative. Instead, I set out to get $1.35.

For a better perspective on my situation, you need to know that literally millions of strangers pass through Union Station, and there is no assurance you'll see the same person twice. In addition, you'll usually find people at heavily traveled locations with schemes for separating honest folks from their hard-earned money.

My *plan* was to secure an easy-to-get, legitimate, collateralized loan. I confidently proceeded to a gift shop where I asked to see the manager. I explained my situation and offered to leave my $100 wristwatch as collateral for a small $1.35 loan which would be repaid the following day.

Apparently the manager had been presented with similar opportunities in the past. He didn't take kindly, nor sympathetically, to my request. He declined to help me and sent me on my way. Now, rejection had been added to my list of troubles.

As I was leaving the store, I heard, "Psst Mister, psst Mister." I turned to see a middle-aged cleaning lady with a pail of water and a mop. She was cleaning the tile floors.

As I approached her, she said, "Mister, how much money did you say you need?" I advised her that the amount was $1.35. She said, "I'll loan you the money. You see, I know what it's like to be broke." Wasn't she *nice*?

She would not take my watch for security, and she requested no other type of assurance that she would be repaid. She took me at my word. She was repaid the following day with cash and an expression of gratitude that exceeded $1.35.

Aren't some people great? That lady is a role model for me. I pass along her kindness as frequently as I can. Have you been kind to someone lately? I recommend it highly. Kindness seems to beget kindness and you usually receive more than you give.

"I Know What It's Like to be Broke."

Airport Ticket Agent

A couple of winters ago, I did an all-day workshop in Minneapolis, Minnesota. The temperature was hovering around zero degrees Fahrenheit and much colder with the wind chill factor. The day before, I had conducted the same workshop in California in 80 degree temperatures.

The travel, lack of sleep, and change in temperature caused me to get laryngitis. When I awoke at 5:30 a.m., I quickly determined that I was in big trouble. The workshop was scheduled to begin at 9 a.m. I check out the room at 7 a.m., and participants usually start arriving about 8:15 a.m.

Registration was large, and I saw no way I could speak the better part of seven hours. Tracking down one of my associates in Kansas, I asked if someone nearby could handle my workshop. I was advised that the closest person who knew my material was in Denver, and there was no way he could get to Minneapolis in time.

In response to my question, "What shall I do?", I was told the company never canceled a workshop. My associate suggested I locate a drug store, purchase a name-brand, high-powered throat spray, and turn my microphone up as loud as it would go. I followed all of the suggestions.

It was a very, very l-o-o-ong day for me and the

participants. However, we made the best of a bad situation. Apparently, the participants felt they received their money's worth. At least no one requested a refund of his registration fee. *Nice* folks!

The true memorable act of kindness occurred after I arrived at the Northwest Airlines check-in counter at the airport. I checked in and went to the waiting room.

The ticket agent summoned me back to the counter and instructed another attendant to upgrade me to first-class. By then, a line was forming behind me, so I quickly thanked the agent and returned to the waiting room.

When all the passengers had been checked in, I again approached the counter. Asking the ticket agent why he had upgraded my flight status, he said, "Mr. Smith, when I heard your voice, I figured you had already had a tough day and that you could probably use a break."

Wasn't that *nice?* He certainly was a perceptive and thoughtful individual. Unfortunately, I didn't get his name. I wanted to write Northwest Airlines and commend them for hiring that person. I won't be in such a hurry the next time.

Little things really do mean a lot! It is amazing how a brief, kind act can overshadow the many hours of misery that preceded it.

"Move Mr. Smith up to First Class."

Pearl Bailey

One evening in New York City, I attended the Broadway play <u>Hello Dolly</u>, starring Pearl Bailey. Miss Bailey had just been released from the hospital that morning, and this would be her first stage appearance in several days.

The concern for her health was such that her doctor attended the play that night and sat in one of the front rows to monitor her condition and be available for medical assistance, if necessary. The play was great. Pearl Bailey performed like the trooper she was.

Throughout the evening, it rained. When the play ended, Miss Bailey caught the attention of one of the ushers and said, "Darlin', is it still raining?" The usher went outside, returned shortly, and said, "Yes, Miss Bailey it is raining pretty hard."

Pearl Bailey then turned to her equally famous co-star, Cab Calloway, and said, "Cab, we can't send these folks out in the rain." They then performed impromptu, entertaining us for about an hour until the rain subsided.

Several hundred people left the theatre that night with a warm feeling for two professionals who demonstrated great love for their work and fellow human beings.

Sometimes one *nice* act affects the lives of hundreds of people. However, one person helped by one kind act is a pretty good return on the investment of the person performing the act.

"We Can't Send These Folks Out in the Rain."

Flight Attendant

Later I tell the story of a trip from Madison, Wisconsin, to Fresno, California. One of the people I met on the Chicago to Los Angeles leg of the trip was a *nice* lady. Her name is Susan. She is a flight attendant.

As she was distributing beverages, I asked her the significance of the bicycle charm she was wearing on a necklace. She replied, "We ride a bicycle built for two. Wait a minute." She then disappeared for a couple of a minutes. When she returned, she handed me a photograph album, and said, "This explains it better." The album contained her wedding pictures. She had been married for 3 weeks and 1 day.

The pictures showed her and her husband, with their bicycle, at various locations in Las Vegas. One picture showed them under an arch at a wedding chapel.

Later I gave Susan one of the $2 bills I carry. Some people think $2 bills are lucky. I inscribed hers, "To Susan and Christopher- Good luck and best wishes! She asked if I carried the $2 bills around looking for women who had been married recently. I replied, "No."

I have no set plan for giving away $2 bills. It is usually based on what strikes me at the moment. However, *nice* people and good deeds usually get my attention. Examples include:

> Susan, Flight attendant - recent marriage
>
> Parents of a newborn baby - seed money for a college fund and to encourage parents to start planning for education
>
> Child reading at the airport - to acknowledge her effort and to encourage her to continue her love for reading
>
> Waitstaff who are pleasant and make my meals more enjoyable
>
> Cab drivers, bus drivers, hotel staff, and other people who are pleasant and/or perform a *nice* gesture that impresses me
>
> My wife - one time, as a token of my appreciation and to let her know that I regard her efforts every bit as highly, and certainly more so, than those of others to whom I give $2 bills

Oh, what about Susan? Three hours into the flight I was engrossed in reading when she passed by my seat. A few moments later, when I put down my paper, I discovered a full glass of <u>warmed</u> mixed nuts on my table tray. Wasn't Susan *nice*? She proved once again - little things do mean a lot.

Little Things Mean A Lot

A Nice Boy

Stories of kindness abound. You need only to be watchful and listen to what is happening around you. Jeanne M. Harper, a friend and professional speaker, e-mailed to me this poem about a little boy. I would gladly credit the author, but at this writing, the poet is unknown.

The Most Beautiful Flower

The park bench was deserted as I sat down to read
Beneath the long, straggly branches of an old willow tree.
Disillusioned by life with good reason to frown,
For the world was intent on dragging me down.

And if that weren't enough to ruin my day,
A young boy out of breath approached me, all tired from play.
He stood right before me with his head tilted down.
And said with great excitement, "Look what I found!"

In his hand was a flower, and what a pitiful sight,
With its petals all worn - not enough rain, or too little light.
Wanting him to take his dead flower and go off to play,
I faked a small smile and then shifted away.

But instead of retreating he sat next to my side
And placed the flower to his nose and declared with overacted surprise,
"It sure smells pretty and it's beautiful, too.
That's why I picked it; here, it's for you."
The weed before me was dying or dead.
Not vibrant of colors: orange, yellow or red.
But I knew I must take it, or he might never leave.
So I reached for the flower and replied, "Just what I need."

But instead of him placing the flower in my hand,
He held it midair without reason or plan.
It was then that I noticed for the very first time
That weed-toting boy could not see: he was blind.

I heard my voice quiver, tears shone in the sun
As I thanked him for picking the very best one.
"You're welcome," he smiled, then ran off to play,
Unaware of the impact he'd had on my day.

I sat there and wondered how he managed to see
A self-pitying woman beneath an old willow tree.
How did he know of my self-indulged plight?
Perhaps from his heart, he'd been blessed with true sight.

Through the eyes of a blind child, at last I could see
The problem was not with the world; the problem was me.
And for all of those times I myself had been blind,
I vowed to see the beauty in life, and appreciate every second that's mine.

And then I held that wilted flower up to my nose,
And breathed in the fragrance of a beautiful rose
And smiled as I watched that young boy, another weed in his hand,
About to change the life of an unsuspecting old man.

Jeanne said to me, "If this message has inspired you, or touched you in any way, or if you feel it can brighten up someone else's day, please forward it."

It touched me. Jeanne and I hope it inspires and touches you and helps brighten your day.

"That's Why I Picked It; Here, It's For You."

WHO ARE YOU?

Are you great?	Are you terrible?
Are you good?	Are you evil?
Are you beautiful?	Are you unattractive?
Are you smart?	Are you dumb?
Are you honest?	Are you dishonest?
Are you friendly?	Are you crabby?
Are you ambitious?	Are you lazy?
Are you positive?	Are you negative?
Are you strong?	Are you weak?
Are you brave?	Are you cowardly?
Are you a help?	Are you a hindrance?

Are you . . . ?

You are who, and what , you think you are!

I'll bet the first column describes you. What do you think?

TRUST

❖

Dan Gable's Mom

If you follow amateur wrestling at all, you most likely have heard of Dan Gable.

During his career, Dan compiled a won-loss record of 64-0 in high school and 118-1 at Iowa State. He won his first 118 college matches before he lost his only match out of the 183 he wrestled in high school and college.

As a high school wrestler in Waterloo, Iowa, he was undefeated and was state champion three times. Wrestling at Iowa State, he was an All-American three times and Big Eight Champion three times.

After college he won titles at the Pan American Games, the Tbilisi Tournament, the World Championships, the Midland Open Championships, and he won a gold medal at the 1972 Summer Olympics.

Dan subsequently became a wrestling coach at the University of Iowa and was appointed head coach in 1977. Since then, his teams (through 1996) have won twenty consecutive Big Ten championships and sixteen NCAA titles.

Remember Dan Gable now?

A few years ago, my son Derek attended one of Dan's wrestling camps at the University of Iowa. I was aware that Russ L. Smith had written a book titled The Legend of Dan Gable "The" Wrestler. I decided to purchase the book, have Dan autograph it, and give it to my son as a surprise and a momento of his wrestling camp experience.

I asked Dan if he had an extra copy of the book, and he said, "No," but that his mother may have a copy at her home in Waterloo, Iowa. I was making sales calls with a company salesmen, and Waterloo was one of our scheduled stops.

When we arrived in Waterloo, we went to the Gable residence. We rang the doorbell and Mrs. Gable came to the door. After the greeting, we introduced ourselves and explained the purpose of our visit. Mrs. Gable said she had copies of the book and she invited us into the house. I looked around the room and made the observation that there certainly was a great number of trophies. Mrs. Gable said there were many more and that a lot of them were with Dan.

Mrs. Gable excused herself and left the room. Soon she returned and said to me, "Here's what most people come to see." With that, she handed me Dan's Olympic Gold Medal.

What an expression of *trust*! We were total strangers whom she had never seen before and whom she most likely would never see again. Yet, she invited us into her home and *entrusted* to us an award that had intrinsic value of hundreds (perhaps thousands) of dollars. It was a prized family possession and the ultimate reward for years of training and hundreds of victories on the wrestling mats.

Yes, Katy Gable showed great *trust* and faith in the honesty of two strangers. I appreciate Katy's courtesy, and her *trust* in us. She helped inspire another young man who was pursuing a dream in wrestling.

"Here's What Most People Come to See."

THANKFULNESS

A Business Man

Examination of a tax return tells you much about the taxpayer. While conducting such an examination with a new client, I made the observation that he was very generous. He asked why I made the statement. I responded that my firm had many clients whose income was much greater than his, but their charitable contributions paled in comparison to his. He said, "There's a story behind that." Since my curiosity was aroused, I asked him to tell me the story.

He was in his sixties and he had led a full and interesting life. His job was in the petroleum industry. He had traveled extensively and met many interesting people.

Although he had a good job in an interesting industry, he had not accumulated much money. He told me that he was an alcoholic and had hardly drawn a sober breath the first 42 years of his life.

Upon returning from a trip, his wife informed him one of the children required medical attention the following week. She gave him money for the health insurance premium. She instructed him to make sure he visited the insurance agent before his office closed or the insurance would lapse. This meant the following week's expenses would not be covered by insurance.

He said, "Walt, I never made it." He didn't need to say any more as I knew the rest of the story.

This man had a loving wife and family. They stuck by him. He joined Alcoholics Anonymous and quit drinking.

He started his own business which has been very successful. In the few years I have known him, annual revenues have increased from a few hundred thousand dollars to several million dollars per year.

One day he visited me before going to the bank to obtain a business loan. He said to me, "I used to be the biggest drunk in my town, and no one would loan me a dime. Today, I'll close a significant loan for my company and it will only require my signature."

After a rocky start in his adult life, this man turned his life around. He doesn't take the credit for his good fortune. He credits his family and his Lord and Savior. He expresses his gratitude by living his faith, generously contributing his company and personal funds to charitable organizations, and remaining active with Alcoholics Anonymous where he shares his story and brings hope to other men and women whose despair he has experienced.

I have never heard his message, but it could very well be, "Never give up. With God's grace, I turned my troubled life around and so can you. Don't quit now."

"Never Give Up . . ."

All's Well That Ends Well

Airplane trips frequently provide interesting experiences. This particular trip is no exception, and it helped to reinforce my belief in the old saying that "all's well that ends well."

The first leg of my trip was from Madison, Wisconsin, to Chicago, Illinois, and from there to Los Angeles, California, with another flight to Fresno, California.

The trip began uneventful enough as I arrived in Madison, from my home 45 miles away, at 8:55 a.m. to catch a flight scheduled to depart at 10:08 a.m. Arrival at Chicago was scheduled for 10:58 a.m. with adequate time for me to catch the 11:44 a.m. departure for Los Angeles.

The Madison flight was on a "puddle jumper" which didn't taxi from the gate until 10:20 a.m. Twelve minutes of my Chicago connecting time already lost! Upon reaching the runway, we sat, and sat, and sat. We later learned that a disabled airplane was blocking our runway. That delay consumed another 20 minutes of valuable connecting time. If the remainder of the flight schedule held, I would have 14 minutes to catch my next plane.

In Chicago, there was a "low-ceiling" and stack up of airplanes. Fortunately, only 5 minutes were lost, so I had roughly 9 minutes once I deplaned. As often happens, our arrival gate was on one concourse and my departure gate was two concourses away. Luckily, the arrival gate was #6 and the departure gate #4, meaning both were near the entrance to each concourse. Toting my 2 carry-on bags, I imitated Jesse Owens and covered the three blocks or so in about 6 minutes.

Upon arrival at gate 4, huffing and puffing, I was told my flight was moved to gate 11. Another hike, and time was running out! However, I was also told that the flight was delayed for about 1 hour -- good news and bad news. The rush was over, but now my California connection was in jeopardy. I breathlessly asked if there were any other flights to Los Angeles.

The gate attendant said, "Yes, but it's at gate 15 (another block away), it's loaded, and it's leaving in 1 minute. You can try to make it if you want." Again - the race was on, and I showed up huffing and puffing.

The flight was delayed a couple of minutes, and I made it! As I write, I have caught my breath, and we are cruising at 35,000 feet trying to get above the storm clouds. The Captain just made an announcement that I found humorous. He said, "We are going higher to avoid the storm, so we all can have a smoother ride." I'm thinking to myself, "Naw, you go ahead and leave me here. I like the excitement of being bounced around."

I have made a few new acquaintances and everything is now going smoothly - proving once again: ALL'S WELL THAT ENDS WELL!

All's Well That Ends Well

LEADERSHIP

A true leader has the confidence to stand alone, the courage to make tough decisions, and the compassion to listen to the needs of others.

TEAM

While a few major accomplishments have been achieved by one person working alone, that is the exception rather than the rule. One person may have a great idea or invention, but refining the thought and converting it to a widely used product or service involves the talents and energy of a supporting cast - a *team*.

I have benefited from *team* efforts in all types of endeavors - social, business, athletic, family, recreational, professional, local, domestic, and international. You name it! There are few projects that can be done more effectively, faster, and better by an individual than they can be performed by a *team*. Plus, teamwork is more fun.

Individually, no synergy exists. One person is restricted by mental and physical limitations. But, with even a *team* of two, one plus one equals something greater than two. That is the result of the ability of two individuals to brainstorm, create, and try ideas that neither person would develop alone.

Since I have witnessed so many successes created by

effective teamwork, I am a die-hard supporter of the *team* concept. To me, the word represents many characteristics that are necessary for the success of any effort.

For the moment, I'll discuss a few characteristics to illustrate my use of "TEAM" as an acronym to remind me of these important concepts.

TRUST - When you are a member of a *team*, it is important that the members *trust* each other. Once a course of action is established, each member must confidently proceed with his or her assignment with absolute *trust* that the other *team* members are carrying out their assignments according to the agreed upon plans and schedules.

You and I can think of many examples to illustrate that concept. It is inherent to every effort that involves two or more people - a *team*.

In some situations, the *trust* and confidence placed in a *team* member is literally a matter of life or death. For starters, think of situations faced by law enforcement officers, fire fighters, military personnel, and other individuals who serve the public in dangerous circumstances.

Although most of us do not face danger of a life or death nature, each of us faces success or failure based upon the effectiveness of our *teams*.

When I assemble a *team*, I place a lot of emphasis on *trust*. When interviewing individuals for key employment opportunities, I stress very heavily my concern about thieves, cheats, and liars. Each of those behaviors destroys confidence and *trust*. *Trust* is needed for a successful *team*.

ENTHUSIASM - A group of individuals working as a *team*, on a project it believes in, will enthusiastically perform its assigned duties. The members will see obstacles as challenges to be overcome. An obstacle will not be a "stop sign" and an excuse for quitting. Instead, it will be seen as a "green light" which sets in motion their creative and physical talents to develop *plans* for bypassing or eliminating the obstacle.

The word *enthusiasm* is derived from a Greek word *entheos*, "en" (in), "theos" (God). I do not know your religious persuasion, and my mission is not to proselytize. However, having a *team* with intense, eager interest plus passion and inspiration (*enthusiasm*) seems like a good idea to me.

Enthusiastic people are upbeat. They think positively. They view setbacks as valuable learning experiences. They have confidence they will prevail in their quests. Their *attitudes* are contagious. They are fun to be around. They bring out the best in themselves and their teammates. Wow, isn't that exciting?

ENERGY - *Trust* and *enthusiasm* generate *energy*. *Energy* is the exertion of an inherent power, the use of one's capacity for vigorous action, and the efficient use of one's power - physical and/or mental.

Awesome results are achieved when the *energy* of *team* members is released in the pursuit of a common goal. For easily identifiable examples, just consider these *teams* - World Series Champions, NBA World Champions, Super Bowl Champions, NASCAR Champions, any space flight, a successful family, academic institutions, police departments, and fire departments.

Think for a moment of the *teams* of which you are a member. Whether we realize it or not, each of us participates in a number of *team* efforts. Now, which of your *teams* expends the most channeled *energy*? Are these the *teams* that are the most successful? Are these the *teams* to which you are drawn? I rest my case.

ACTION - We may have very lofty *hopes and dreams.* However, if we do not act to change them to reality, we are merely "hopers" and "dreamers." Nothing changes!

It is encouraging to know that *hopes and dreams* can come true. It happens everyday to someone, somewhere. Why not you? Throughout this book, you'll find an outline of *actions* you can take, and principles you can follow, to transform your *hopes and dreams* from fantasyland to the real world where you will find more enjoyment and benefits.

What is better: To dream of having a million dollars or to have a million dollars? To hope for improved health or to have good health? To hope for sobriety or to be sober? To dream of a happy marriage or to be happily married? To hope for a better job or to have a better job? To dream of world travel or to travel the world?

What do you hope and dream about? Help is all around you. Family members, friends, pastors, employers, social workers, professionals of all types, and other people have already acquired what you want and done what you want to do.

In addition, thousands of books, tapes, seminars, workshops, courses at educational institutions, and other resources can be tapped.   The bottom line is that you must do something - take *action*.   In my pocket, I carry a coin which is a constant reminder to me that to achieve results, I must take *action*.

On the front of the coin is a skeletonized image of "The Thinker."   The inscription reads, "ACT NOW, HE WHO HESITATES IS LOST."

On the back of the coin are the names of James E. Delaney who created the coin and George W. Cecil who wrote the following inscription which appears on the coin:

"On the Plains
of hesitation bleach

the bones of countless
millions who, at the

dawn of Victory,

Sat down to wait,
and waiting -
died."

Pretty thought provoking isn't it? I urge you to take *action* on your *hopes and dreams.* Do not let them wither, die, and bleach on the plains of hesitation. ACT NOW!

MARVELOUS RESULTS - These are the culmination of all your *planning, practice, patience, persistence, attitude, impressions, nice deeds, trust, enthusiasm, energy, and action.*

They are your reward for a job well done. Of course, you don't stop now. Instead, you start the process over as you tackle new or yet unfulfilled *hopes and dreams.*

The word "TEAM" as an acronym.

       T -   TRUST

       E -   ENTHUSIASM AND ENERGY

       A -   ACTION

       M -   MARVELOUS RESULTS
                      ©1995

Assemble your *teams* to help you realize your *hopes and dreams*. If you have a number of well-meaning people who love you, believe in your commitment and sincerity of purpose, want you to succeed, and are willing to help you - your success is practically assured. Go for it!

BE SWIFT TO ACT

An eagle soars,

 an eagle hovers

Until its prey

 it does discover.

Then dropping swiftly

 from the sky,

It lands its catch

 in the blink of an eye.

Like the eagle, we must be keen of vision and prepared to "seize the moment" when the opportunity arises.

COMMITMENT

Never doubt that a small group of thoughtful committed citizens can change the world.

--Margaret Mead

FINAL SUGGESTIONS

You may have noticed that you can spell the word "PAINT" by combining the first letter of each chapter heading. Use this acronym to easily remember the formula for making your *hopes and dreams* come true.

P - PLANNING, PRACTICE, PATIENCE, PERSISTENCE

A - ATTITUDE

I - IMPRESSIONS, INTEGRITY

N - NICE

T - TRUST, THANKFULNESS, TEAM

Paint your *hopes and dreams* on the movie screen of your mind. This is frequently called visualization. From time to time, roll the mental images of your *hopes and dreams*. Measure the progress you are making towards transforming them to reality.

Do you have a *plan*? Is your *team* in place? Are you making reasonable progress? Are you on schedule? Have your priorities changed? If so, have you revised your goals and timetables for realizing your *hopes and dreams*?

The course of life is always changing. The winds of change, challenge, and opportunity regularly alter our *hopes and dreams*. That is why we must constantly determine where we are, where we want to be, and how we are going to get there.

MY DREAM FOR YOU

I am frequently asked why I am so upbeat. I respond that I am a very blest fellow. So many of my *hopes and dreams* have come true that I sometimes feel I have received more than my fair share. That's where "giving back" becomes important in life.

With this book, I want to stimulate your thoughts and actions toward the realization of your *hopes and dreams.* The process is not rocket science. It's just a matter of implementing the time-tested principles illustrated in this book and taking *action* in the form of dedicated, committed effort.

Good luck and God speed as you pursue your *hopes and dreams.*

Keep Soaring!

DREAM

You see things as they are and ask, "Why?" I dream things that never were and ask, "Why not?"

--George Bernard Shaw

Dream, plan, and do - your dreams will come true.

T. CARRERO

On the edge of the ledge an eaglet stands
    for it is time to fly.
For that mighty bird has a destiny and
    so my Lord have I.
As the eagle is not content to stay
    at levels safe,
So I, on the edge of the ledge
    await Thy will.
Lord, I was meant to fly.

- Robert A. Schuller[1]

---

[1]Power to Grow Beyond Yourself, Fleming H. Revell Company.

Copies of this book may be obtained by writing to the address or calling the phone number below.

1-5 copies	$9.95 each + $3.00 S&H
6-10 copies	$8.95 each + $5.00 S&H
11-25 copies	$7.95 each (S&H included)
26-50 copies	$7.45 each (S&H included)
50+ copies	$6.95 each (S&H included)

Arrangements for keynote speeches, workshops, or consulting services can be made by contacting Walt Smith at:

102 Fourth Avenue
Baraboo, WI 53913
608/356-7733 phone
608/356-7735 fax
waltsmith@midplains.net

Walt's major keynote speeches are -

"Hopes and Dreams" - Motivational and inspirational

"Land of the Free and Home of the Brave" - Patriotic

Standardized and customized four to eight hour workshops help business owners and managers answer such questions as:

Is my business/department making money?

Is my business/department making as much money as it should?

Do I really know if my business/department is making money?

Do I have adequate controls to safeguard the assets for which I am responsible?

How can I create and implement realistic plans and monitor results to achieve my goals?

- and much more!